Post your finished work and join the community.
#FAITHINCOLOR

THE PROMISES OF GOD

COLOR as You Reflect on God's Words to You

PASSIO

A person who wholly follows the Lord is one

who believes that the promises of God are trustworthy, that

He is with His people, and that they are well able to overcome.

—WATCHMAN NEE

You Can Trust God's Promises

God knows you, and He knows what you need. He has provided promises in His Word that give assurance and direction for every situation you face. These promises from God's Word, combined with the beautiful artwork in this coloring book, will provide peace and hope as you let go of fear, worry, and anxiety and trust that God's promises are true.

Don't miss the short quotations placed on the facing page of each design. Each one was chosen to complement the illustration while reminding you of the precious promises God makes to us in His Word. As you color each design, you might want to reflect quietly on each verse or even say a prayer. Like many people, you may find that the cares and worries of life melt away as you focus your thoughts on God's many promises to protect, heal, save, and keep you.

Think back to times in your past when God has kept His promises and brought you through a hopeless situation or tough problem. Record these memories in this book or a journal. Remembering God's faithfulness will build your faith that He is able to meet every need that you face now or in your future. You can trust Him. And when you do, His peace, "which surpasses all understanding, will protect your hearts and minds through Christ Jesus" (Phil. 4:7).

It might interest you to know that the quotations in this book are taken from the Modern English Version of the Holy Bible. The Modern English Version (MEV) is the most modern translation produced in the King James tradition within the last thirty years. This formal equivalence translation maintains the beauty of the past yet provides fresh clarity for a new generation of Bible readers. If you would like more information on the MEV, please visit www.mevbible.com.

We hope you find this coloring book to be both beautiful and inspirational. And as you color, remember that the best artistic endeavors have no rules. Unleash your creativity as you experiment with colors, textures, and mediums. Freedom of self-expression will help to release wellness, balance, mindfulness, and inner peace into your life, allowing you to enjoy the process as well as the finished product. When you're finished, you can frame your favorite creations for displaying or gift giving.

For I know the plans that I have for you, says the LORD,

plans for peace and not for evil, to give you a future and a hope.

—JEREMIAH 29:11, MEV

For I am persuaded that neither death nor life, neither angels nor principalities nor powers, neither things present nor things to come, neither height nor depth, nor any other created thing, shall be able to separate us from the love of God, which is in Christ Jesus our Lord.

—ROMANS 8:38–39, MEV

I can do all things because of Christ who strengthens me.

—PHILIPPIANS 4:13, MEV

And He said, "My Presence will go with you,

and I will give you rest."

—Exodus 33:14, MEV

You shall know the truth, and the truth shall set you free.

—*John 8:32*, MEV

For God has not given us the spirit of fear, but

of power, and love, and self-control.

—2 TIMOTHY 1:7, MEV

But seek first the kingdom of God and His righteousness, and

all these things shall be given to you.

—MATTHEW 6:33, MEV

There is therefore now no condemnation for those who are in Christ Jesus, who walk not according to the flesh, but according to the Spirit.

—ROMANS 8:1, MEV

Come to Me, all you who labor and are heavily burdened, and I will give you rest. Take My yoke upon you, and learn from Me. For I am meek and lowly in heart, and you will find rest for your souls.

—MATTHEW 11:28–29, MEV

Write your favorite promise verse inside the heart on the next page.

But my God shall supply your every need according

to His riches in glory by Christ Jesus.

—Philippians 4:19, MEV

For He is our peace, who has made both groups one

and has broken down the barrier of the dividing wall.

—EPHESIANS 2:14, MEV

The LORD is good, a stronghold in the day of distress; and

He knows those who take refuge in Him.

—*NAHUM 1:7, MEV*

Remember, I am with you, and I will protect you wherever you go, and I will bring you back to this land. For I will not leave you until I have done what I promised you.

—Genesis 28:15, MEV

God is able to make all grace abound toward you, so

that you, always having enough of everything,

may abound to every good work.

—2 Corinthians 9:8, MEV

The Lord's...compassions do not fail. They are new every morning; great is Your faithfulness.

—Lamentations 3:22–23, MEV

No weapon that is formed against you shall prosper, and every tongue that shall rise against you in judgment, you shall condemn. This is the heritage of the servants of the LORD, and their vindication is from Me, says the LORD.

—ISAIAH 54:17, MEV

For since the beginning of the world men

have not heard, nor perceived by ear, neither has

the eye seen a God besides You, who acts

for the one who waits for Him.

—*Isaiah 64:4*, MEV

Now to Him who is able to do exceedingly abundantly

beyond all that we ask or imagine, according to

the power that works in us, to Him be the glory

in the church and in Christ Jesus throughout all

generations, forever and ever. Amen.

—*EPHESIANS 3:20–21, MEV*

We know that all things work together for

good to those who love God, to those who are

called according to His purpose.

—Romans 8:28, mev

*Oh, taste and see that the L*ORD *is good; blessed*

is the man who takes refuge in Him.

—P*SALM* 34:8, *MEV*

The heavens declare the glory of God, and

the firmament shows His handiwork.

—*PSALM 19:1, MEV*

Therefore He says: "Awake, you who sleep, arise from the dead, and Christ will give you light."

—EPHESIANS 5:14, MEV

From the end of the earth I will cry to You; when my

heart faints, lead me to the rock that is higher than I.

—PSALM 61:2, MEV

For He satisfies the longing soul and fills

the hungry soul with goodness.

—Psalm 107:9, MEV

And this is the promise that He has

promised us—eternal life.

—1 JOHN 2:25, MEV

I will lift up my eyes to the hills, from where does

my help come? My help comes from the LORD,

who made heaven and earth.

—PSALM 121:1–2, MEV

Are not two sparrows sold for a penny? And not

one of them will fall to the ground without your

Father. But the very hairs of your head are

all numbered. Therefore do not fear. You are

more valuable than many sparrows.

—MATTHEW 10:29–31, MEV

Trust in the LORD with all your heart, and lean not on your

own understanding; in all your ways acknowledge Him,

and He will direct your paths.

—PROVERBS 3:5–6, MEV

I am with you always, even to the end of the age.

—Matthew 28:20, MEV

*Return to the L*ORD *your God, for He is*

gracious and merciful, slow to anger, and

abounding in steadfast love.

—J*OEL* 2:13, MEV

Know therefore that the LORD *your God,*

He is God, the faithful God, who keeps covenant

and mercy with them who love Him and keep His

commandments to a thousand generations.

—DEUTERONOMY 7:9, MEV

Peace I leave with you. My peace I give to you. Not as the world gives do I give to you. Let not your heart be troubled, neither let it be afraid.

—JOHN 14:27, MEV

Have not I commanded you? Be strong and courageous. Do not be afraid or dismayed, for the Lord your God is with you wherever you go.

—Joshua 1:9, MEV

You will make known to me the path of life; in Your

presence is fullness of joy; at Your right hand

there are pleasures for evermore.

—PSALM *16:11,* mev

For this reason we do not lose heart: Even though our outward man is perishing, yet our inward man is being renewed day by day. Our light affliction, which lasts but for a moment, works for us a far more exceeding and eternal weight of glory, while we do not look at the things which are seen, but at the things which are not seen. For the things which are seen are temporal, but the things which are not seen are eternal.

—2 Corinthians 4:16–18, MEV

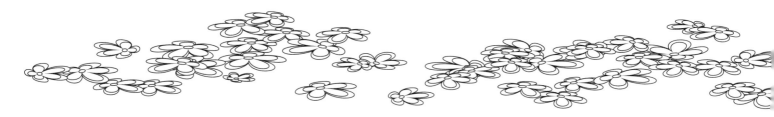

*The L*ORD *your God is in your midst, a Mighty One,*

who will save. He will rejoice over you with

gladness, He will renew you with His love,

He will rejoice over you with singing.

—Z*EPHANIAH* 3:17, MEV

But He said to me, "My grace is sufficient for you, for My strength is made perfect in weakness." Therefore most gladly I will boast in my weaknesses, that the power of Christ may rest upon me.

—2 CORINTHIANS 12:9, MEV

For the LORD *gives wisdom; out of His mouth come knowledge and understanding. He lays up sound wisdom for the righteous; He is a shield to those who walk uprightly. He keeps the paths of justice, and preserves the way of His saints.*

—PROVERBS 2:6–8, MEV

But those who wait upon the LORD shall renew their strength;

they shall mount up with wings as eagles, they shall run and not

be weary, and they shall walk and not faint.

—*ISAIAH 40:31, MEV*

Now the Lord is the Spirit. And where the

Spirit of the Lord is, there is liberty.

—2 CORINTHIANS 3:17, MEV

*A man's heart devises his way, but the L*ORD *directs his steps.*

—P*ROVERBS* 16:9, MEV

You are of God, little children, and have overcome them,

because He who is in you is greater than he who is in the world.

—*1 JOHN 4:4, MEV*

I will both lie down in peace and sleep; for You,

LORD, make me dwell safely and securely.

—PSALM 4:8, MEV

But Jesus looked at them and said, "With men this is impossible, but with God all things are possible."

—Matthew 19:26, MEV

Most CHARISMA HOUSE BOOK GROUP products are available at special quantity discounts for bulk purchase for sales promotions, premiums, fund-raising, and educational needs. For details, write Charisma House Book Group, 600 Rinehart Road, Lake Mary, Florida 32746, or telephone (407) 333-0600.

THE PROMISES OF GOD published by Passio
Charisma Media/Charisma House Book Group
600 Rinehart Road
Lake Mary, Florida 32746
www.charismahouse.com

Unless otherwise noted, all Scripture quotations are taken from the Holy Bible, Modern English Version. Copyright © 2014 by Military Bible Association. Used by permission. All rights reserved.

Design Director: Justin Evans
Cover Design: Justin Evans
Interior Design: Justin Evans, Lisa Rae McClure, Vincent Pirozzi

Illustrations: Getty Images / Depositphotos

Watchman Nee quote taken from *God's Keeping Power* (Anaheim, CA: Living Stream Ministry, 1993), 3.

International Standard Book Number: 978-1-62998-774-3

16 17 18 19 20 — 987

Printed in the United States of America